rockschool®

Hot Rock
Guitar Grade 1

8 classic rock tracks specially edited for Grade 1
for use in Rockschool examinations

www.rockschool.co.uk

Acknowledgements

Published by Rockschool Ltd. © 2014 under license from Music Sales Ltd
Catalogue Number RSK041401
ISBN: 978-1-908920-40-9

AUDIO
Produced by Tom Farncombe, Music Sales Ltd
Engineered, mixed and mastered by Jonas Persson, Music Sales Ltd

MUSICIANS
Dave Cottrell, Arthur Dick, Tom Fleming, Tom Fleming, Paul Honey, Noam Lederman, Brett Morgan, Jonas Persson, Ian Thomas, Paul Townsend

PUBLISHING
Compiled and edited by James Uings, Simon Pitt, Simon Troup and Jeremy Ward
Layout, internal design and music engraving by Simon and Jennie Troup, Digital Music Art
Cover designed by Philip Millard, Philip Millard Design
Audio and photographic copyright notices can be found at the back of the book

PRINTING
Printed and bound in the United Kingdom by Caligraving Ltd
Media hosting by Dropcards Inc

DISTRIBUTION
Exclusive Distributors: Music Sales Ltd

CONTACTING ROCKSCHOOL
www.rockschool.co.uk
Telephone: +44 (0)845 460 4747
Fax: +44 (0)845 460 1960

Table of Contents

Introductions & Information

Page

Rockschool Grade Pieces

Page

Additional Information

Page

Welcome to Hot Rock Guitar Grade 1

Welcome to Hot Rock Guitar Grade 1. This book of classic and contemporary tracks has been compiled to give you a resource to help you develop your guitar and performance skills.

Songs

Hot Rock Guitar Grade 1 contains eight songs that cover a wide range of styles and artists of the last 40 years. The songs can be used as Free Choice Pieces in the Rockschool Guitar Grade 1 exam – see page 40 for more information on the preparing for and entering Rockschool exams. The songs can also be used in the performance units in public exams such as GCSEs. You can also enjoy playing them for their own sake, broadening your repertoire and learning many popular riffs and chord sequences in the process.

The songs in this book are arrangements of the original songs. While adjustments have been made to make the pieces playable at Grade 1 and to make them appropriate as examination pieces, we have worked hard to maintain the integrity and spirit of the original music.

Each song is printed over 2 pages and is preceded by a Fact File detailing information about the original recording, the band and the guitarist who played on it and some recommended listening if you wish to research the artist further. At the end of each chapter there is a Walkthrough which gives you tips on how to play the exam arrangement and any technical challenges to look out for as you practise the song.

Audio

Each song in Hot Rock Guitar has two audio tracks that can be downloaded via the download card that comes with the book. The first is a full track that includes the guitar part and a full band. The other is a backing track with the guitar taken off so you can play along with the band. The backing tracks should be used in examinations.

The audio files are supplied in mp3 format, the most widely compatible audio format in common usage – mp3s will likely be familiar to anyone with a computer, iPod, smartphone or similar device. Once downloaded you will be able to play them on any compatible device; we hope that you find this extra versatility useful.

Download Cards

Download cards are easy to use, simply go to *www.dropcards.com/hotrock* and type in the code on the back of your card. It's best to do this where you have a good connection so the download is uninterrupted. If for any reason you have a problem with your download please contact *www.dropcards.com/help* who will resolve any issues you may have.

Please note that most tablets and smartphones (including the iPad, iPhone and many Android-based devices) do not allow files to be downloaded directly on to the device. On the iPad and iPhone, files need to be downloaded to the Mac or PC first, then synced to the device using the iTunes application. Operating systems for mobile devices are updated frequently, so ensure you consult the most recent documentation available for your device and operating system for further details.

Tone

We have also included some general advice on getting an authentic tone for each track, including suggested amp settings. Treat these as a guide to point you in the right direction rather than a strict set of instructions that must be followed slavishly: guitar and amplifier sounds differ significantly, so the right setup for one guitar may not be the correct setup for another. Your ears should always be the final judge about whether something sounds good or not. If you require more information on amplifiers and their controls, pickups and guitar tones in general, please refer to our Introduction To Tone on pages 38 and 39.

We hope that you enjoy playing these pieces. You can find further details about Rockschool's guitar and other instrumental syllabuses by visiting our website at *www.rockschool.co.uk*.

SONG TITLE: CHASING CARS
ALBUM: EYES OPEN
RELEASED: 2006
LABEL: POLYDOR
GENRE: INDIE

PERSONNEL: GARY LIGHTBODY (VOX+GTR)
NATHAN CONNOLLY (GTR)
PAUL WILSON (BASS)
JONNY QUINN (DRUMS)
TOM SIMPSON (KEYS)

UK CHART PEAK: 6
US CHART PEAK: 5

BACKGROUND INFO

'Chasing Cars' is the second single from Snow Patrol's 2006 album *Eyes Open*. It is a based on a single three-chord progression, but 'Chasing Cars' is far from simple. The song starts with a sparse picked eighth-note guitar line which is augmented by subtle keyboard parts. The arrangement uses changes in dynamics to develop the song. The third chorus sees 'Chasing Cars' move up another notch adding drums and several distorted guitars playing different inversions (where the notes of a chord are arranged in a different order) to create an orchestra-like wall of guitars. The end of the song sees the song return to its sparse beginnings with the re-stating of the simple picked guitar part.

THE BIGGER PICTURE

Snow Patrol's rise to super-stardom has been slow and steady with their first top ten hit ('Run') coming in 2004, six years after the release of their first album. They have grown to become one of the most successful British indie acts of the last decade and even have the dubious distinction of a reality TV winner, Leona Lewis, achieving a UK number 1 with her cover of 'Run'.

NOTES

Although it didn't achieve a number 1 in the UK or the U.S. 'Chasing Cars' still receives massive airplay and can be heard almost constantly in TV shows. A moving acoustic version of 'Chasing Cars' appears on the soundtrack for the US TV show *Grey's Anatomy*.

RECOMMENDED LISTENING

Snow Patrol's songs are masterpieces of arrangement and see the guitar adopting a supporting role on their songs rather than the dominant riffs and extended guitar solos you might expect to hear from a rock, blues or metal band. Their other mega-hit is 'Run'. A single from their third album, 2004's *Final Straw*. It starts with the same understated feel as 'Chasing Cars', based primarily on a simple guitar riff before moving to a dramatic, perfectly crafted chorus. 'Set Fire To The Third Bar' from 2006's *Eyes Open* has an earthy rhythm and some subtle acoustic and electric guitar playing. It also features Martha Wainwright on vocals.

Chasing Cars

Snow Patrol

Words & Music by Gary Lightbody, Nathan Connolly,
Tom Simpson, Paul Wilson & Jonathan Quinn

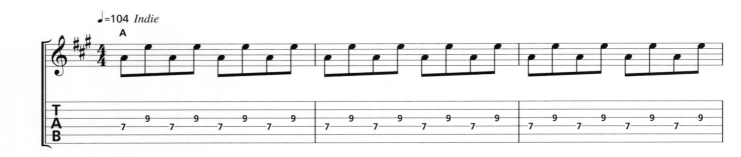

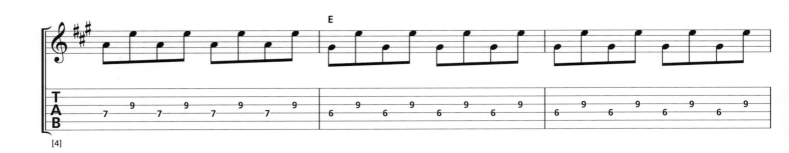

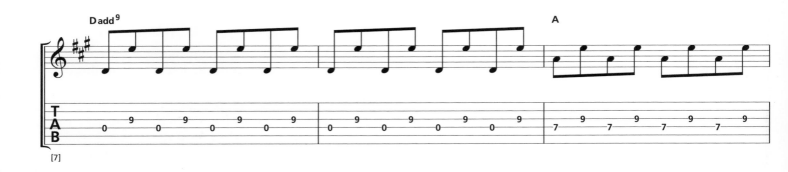

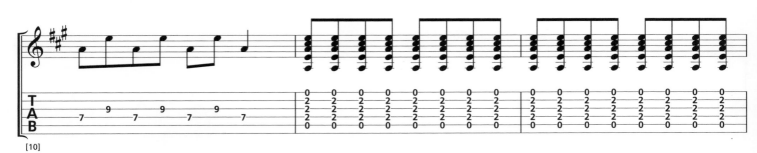

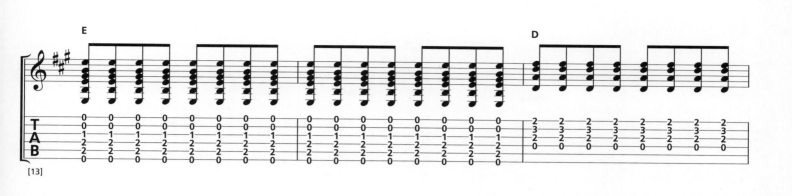

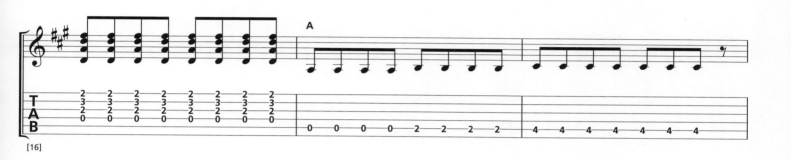

Walkthrough

Tone

The original version of 'Chasing Cars' features lots of guitars using a variety of different tones layered on top of each other to produce a wall of sound. For the exam version you need to create a tone that contains elements of all these sounds. Select a light overdrive that sounds almost completely clean in the intro and verse sections but is only slightly distorted when you strum (which will be naturally louder) in the chorus section.

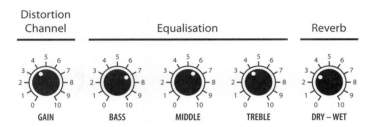

Intro/Verse 1 (Bars 1–10)

The intro consists of a two-note pattern based on an A5 powerchord. This pattern continues in the verse and develops to follow a three-chord progression that's the basis of the whole song.

Bars 1–10 | *Consistent picking*

This pattern looks deceptively simple. Aside from playing the correct notes you will need to focus on striking the strings with the same force every time to maintain a consistent, even sound.

Bar 7 | *Open and fretted strings*

The challenge of these two bars is to keep the open string's volume consistent with the fretted note. An open string naturally has more resonance than a fretted one so you will need to strike them more lightly to maintain consistency.

Chorus (Bars 11–18)

The chorus consists of open chords strummed in an eighth-note pattern. The final two bars are an ascending single note part that leads back into the verse.

Bars 11–16 | *Consistent strumming*

The strummed sections can be played with either all down strokes or alternating up and down strokes. Using all down strokes (Fig. 1) gives a more even, consistent sound, but some guitarists may find it hard to maintain at this tempo. Alternate strumming (Fig. 2) has a less consistent sound, but is potentially easier to achieve at tempo and can therefore sound more fluent. Experiment with both to see which you prefer. Whichever technique you decide to use, you should maintain throughout – switching between them mid-song may affect the performance.

Bars 11–16 | *Changing chords*

The best way to become faster at changing chords is to 'drill' the changes. Play each chord with a single strum and then move to the next chord. Repeat this several times for the whole progression. Start slowly and make sure you play each chord accurately without fret buzz or dead notes and gradually increase the speed.

Bars 17–18 | *Single note picking*

These notes can be played using all down strokes, but alternate picking (down-up-down-up) is a more efficient motion which produces a more fluent sound. It's a good technique to have at your disposal when you come to play more challenging songs.

Verse 2 (Bars 19–27)

This verse is based on one of the other guitar parts played in the heavily layered original arrangement. It uses two-note chords played in eighth notes.

Bars 19–27 | *Strumming the high strings*

Unlike the strummed and picked sections earlier in the song it's much harder to get a fluent sound using an alternate strumming action as there's a tendency to strike one string at a time - the lowest sounding string on the down stroke and the highest on the up stroke.

Bars 23–23 | *Fretting accuracy*

Make sure you play these notes with your thumb behind the neck and on the tips of your fingers. This will ensure your third finger doesn't accidentally mute the first string. Pick each note individually to make sure they ring out clearly.

Fig. 1: Consistent Strumming – All down strokes

Fig. 2: Consistent Strumming – Up and down strokes

SONG TITLE: JAILBREAK
ALBUM: JAILBREAK
RELEASED: 1976
LABEL: VERTIGO
GENRE: CLASSIC ROCK

PERSONNEL: PHIL LYNOTT (BASS+VOX)
SCOTT GORHAM (GTR)
BRIAN ROBERTSON (GTR)
BRIAN DOWNEY (DRUMS)

UK CHART PEAK: 31
US CHART PEAK: N/A

BACKGROUND INFO

The title track from 1976's *Jailbreak* was the first single. As with many Thin Lizzy songs, the verse's tasteful, choppy guitar riff serves to support bassist/vocalist Phil Lynott's off-the-cuff vocal delivery. In the chorus the rhythm guitar takes even more of a back seat playing simple sustained chords while two lead guitars add high register licks throughout. There are also lead licks before each verse which make use of a wah wah pedal. Unusually for a Thin Lizzy track, 'Jailbreak' features very little harmony guitar.

THE BIGGER PICTURE

While Wishbone Ash guitarists Andy Powell and Ted Turner should receive credit for their twin guitar innovations, Thin Lizzy's twin axe attack had a huge impact on the guitar world, influencing many bands, including metal giants Metallica, Iron Maiden and The Darkness. Metallica recorded their own version of Thin Lizzy's 'Whiskey In The Jar', converting the famous melody line into a heavy metal riff.

NOTES

Aside from the 'Jailbreak' guitar duo of Scott Gorham and Brian Robertson, blues/rock icon Gary Moore also spent time in the Thin Lizzy line up. After two short periods with the band in the mid 1970s, he recorded and contributed to the writing of 1979's *Black Rose: A Rock Legend* teaming up with Scott Gorham on guitar duties. Moore has performed his own version of 'Don't Believe A Word', which begins as a slower tempo blues before reverting to the original, uptempo rock feel.

RECOMMENDED LISTENING

1976's *Jailbreak* contains some of Thin Lizzy's best guitar work. 'The Boys Are Back In Town' is their most famous song and the harmonised melody is a fine example of their twin guitar sound. 'The Cowboy Song' is another excellent harmonised riff. Elsewhere, 'Emerald' features an extended trade off outro solo between Gorham and Robertson. Another classic Thin Lizzy moment is their version of the Irish folk song 'Whiskey In The Jar'. Aside from the catchy melodies throughout the song, there's also the free time solo guitar intro and the perfectly crafted melodic solo.

Jailbreak

Thin Lizzy
Words & Music by Phil Lynott

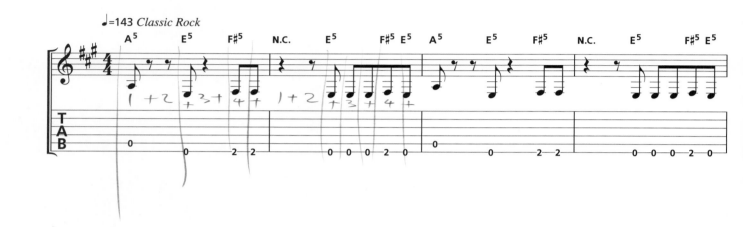

[5]

[9]

[13]

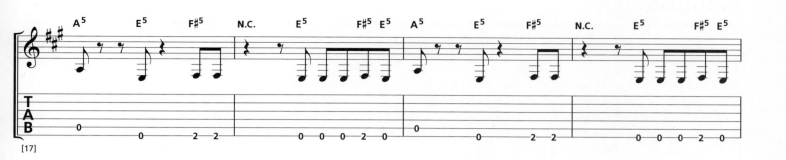

[17]

[21]

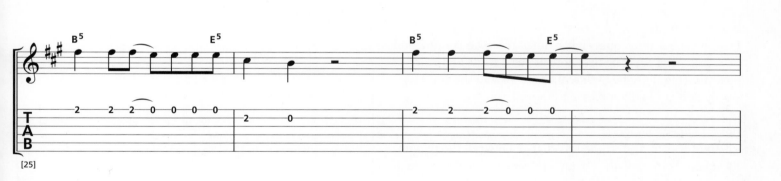

[25]

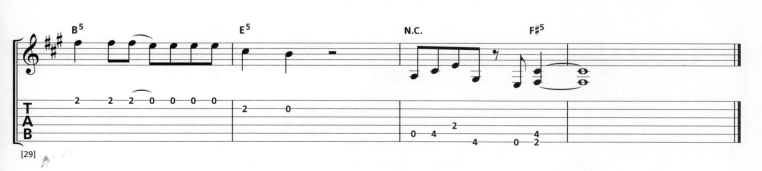

[29]

Walkthrough

Tone

The original version of this song was played on the classic rock setup of a Gibson Les Paul played through a Marshall amplifier. If you don't own a guitar with humbuckers use the neck pickup to get a thicker tone. Make sure your sound isn't too distorted: you're looking for an overdriven sound that 'breaks up' when the guitar is played aggressively rather than full-on distortion that will turn the sound to mush.

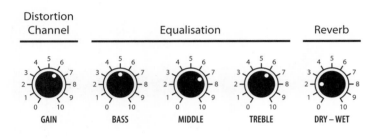

Intro (Bars 1–8)

The first half of this tight, snappy riff uses single notes on the fifth and sixth strings. The second half is a variation that uses two-note powerchords.

Bar 1 | *Muting*

The key to this riff is to make sure the notes ring for the correct duration. To mute the eighth notes, simultaneously place your pick and the edge of your picking hand on the string after striking the note.

Bar 2 | *Up beats*

Divide the bar into equal eighth notes and then count aloud "1 & 2 & 3 & 4 &". The first note of bar 2 starts on the '&' of beat two (Fig. 1). The high tempo means you should start slowly and gradually increase the speed.

Bar 6 | *Quick Changes*

The best way to perfect the fast change between the E^5 and $F\#^5$ chord is to 'drill' the changes by repeatedly playing each chord once then moving to the next.

Bar 8 | *Counting Rests*

You must count the rests in this 'empty' bar to help you play the first chord of the chorus in time. Count "1 2 3 4" through the bar then play the first chord of the chorus where the next '1' would be.

Chorus (Bars 9–16)

This section is built on sustained chords, some of which are 'pushed' (*i.e.* they start on the last eighth note of the previous bar) and some are preceded by a quick eighth note. The section ends with a challenging single-note riff.

Bar 9 | *Pushes*

The first E^5 chord of the chorus starts on the 'and' of beat 4 and continues into the next bar. Count "1 & 2 & 3 & 4 &" and play the chord on the correct beat. Start slowly and gradually increase the speed.

Verse (Bars 17–24)

This section is similar to the intro consisting of the same single-note riff followed by powerchords formula, but features the first note of the chorus at the end of the last bar instead of a full bar's rest.

Chorus 2 (Bars 25–32)

This version of the chorus is single notes based on Phil Lynott's original vocal melody. It's played in open position (the open strings and first four frets or the guitar) and concludes with the same riff as the first chorus.

Bar 25 | *Pull-offs*

The pull-off is indicated by the curved line joining the third and fourth notes of the bar (Fig. 2). Play the first note and, without picking, pull your finger off the string towards the floor in a snapping motion.

Bar 31 | *Correct note values*

The final chord lasts for five beats. A guitar with a distorted tone can sustain for a long time, so you'll need to stop the strings from ringing at the appropriate point.

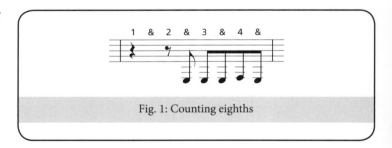

Fig. 1: Counting eighths

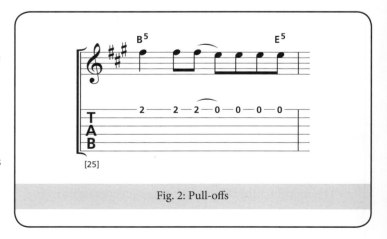

Fig. 2: Pull-offs

```
SONG TITLE:  LIVING ON A PRAYER
    ALBUM:   SLIPPERY WHEN WET
 RELEASED:   1986
    LABEL:   MERCURY RECORDS
    GENRE:   POP ROCK


PERSONNEL:   JON BON JOVI (VOX)
             RICHIE SAMBORA (GTR)
             ALEC JOHN SUCH (BASS)
             TICCO TORRES (DRUMS)


UK CHART PEAK:  4
US CHART PEAK:  1
```

BACKGROUND INFO

'Living On A Prayer' was the second single from Bon Jovi's 1986 release *Slippery When Wet* and is by far their biggest hit. It remains a dancefloor sing-along and is the climax to many a Bon Jovi stadium show. The guitar parts in 'Living On A Prayer' are quite simple and play a supporting role to the vocal line. The distinctive repeated main riff (augmented with a distinctive voice box effect) chugs along behind the verses and the pre-chorus guitar part closely follows the rhythm of the vocal melody. These devices keep the song's arrangement uncluttered and allows the listener to focus on the melodies – one of the main reasons 'Living On A Prayer' is now considered a *bona-fide* classic.

THE BIGGER PICTURE

While their early releases *Bon Jovi* and *7800° Fahrenheit* achieved some critical acclaim, it was *Slippery When Wet* that heralded the start of Bon Jovi's golden era. They enlisted producer Bruce Fairbain (his contribution earned him big production jobs with the likes of Aerosmith and Poison) who helped shape the band's ultra radio-friendly sound. They also enlisted the services of songwriter Desmond Child. Child had huge success writing and co-writing hits for KISS, Heart, Alice Cooper and Aerosmith. He co-wrote four songs on *Slippery When Wet*, most significantly their two biggest hits: 'You Give Love A Bad Name' and, of course, 'Living On A Prayer'. He also co-wrote four songs on *New Jersey* including the fan favourite, 'Bad Medicine'.

NOTES

The Springsteen-style 'hope in the face of adversity' lyrics are a theme that Jon Bon Jovi has drawn on throughout his career. 'Born To Be My Baby' (from *New Jersey*) and 'Someday I'll Be Saturday Night' (from *These Days*) all owe a debt, lyrically at least, to The Boss's classic tunes, particularly 'The River'.

RECOMMENDED LISTENING

Bon Jovi and *7800° Fahrenheit* are solid efforts, but *Slippery When Wet* and *New Jersey* are where the real Bon Jovi quality lies. Aside from the tracks already mentioned, 'Let It Rock' and 'Social Disease' from *Slippery…* are essential listening and 'Lay Your Hands On Me' and 'Bad Medicine' are among the best tracks on *New Jersey*.

Living On A Prayer

Bon Jovi

Words & Music by Jon Bon Jovi, Richie Sambora & Desmond Child

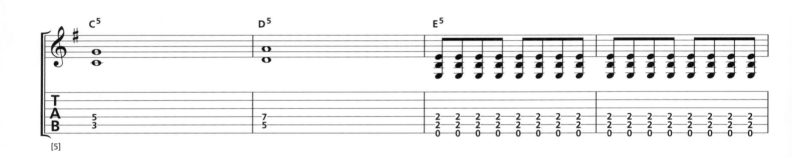

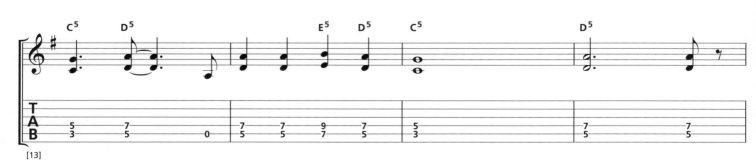

Hot Rock Guitar Grade 1

14

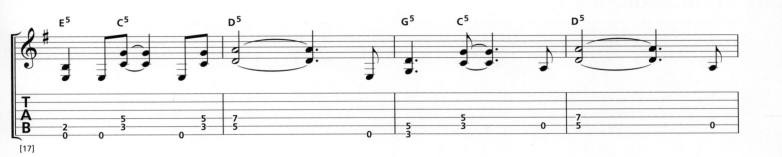

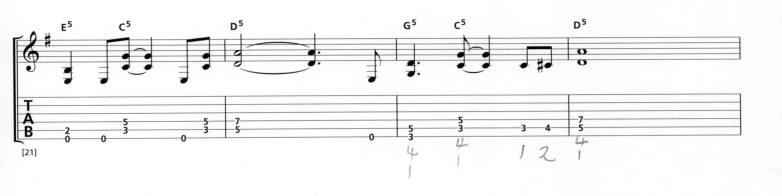

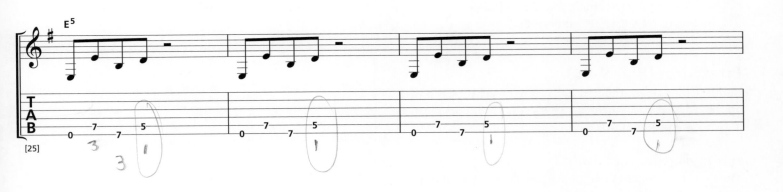

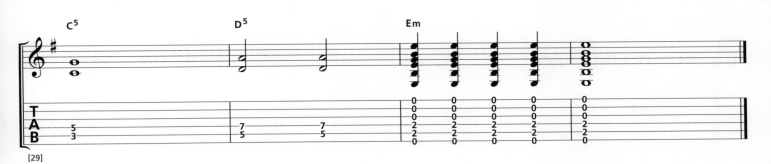

Walkthrough

Tone

The original version of this song uses a voice box effect for the main riff, but the rest of the guitar parts on this track feature a modern hi-gain sound that is 'distortion' rather than 'overdrive'. This kind of tone is typical of rock music of this era. At Grade 1 you are not expected to use any effects, so aim for a full, thick sound that's quite distorted, but still has clarity.

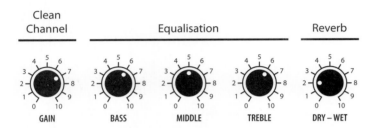

Verse (Bars 1–8)

The first four bars are an E^5 powerchord played in an eighth note rhythm. The two remaining chords of the progression are sustained powerchords. The section finishes with a lower three-note version of the E^5 powerchord.

Bars 1–8 | *Powerchord fingerings*
You can play the powerchords with either the first and third or the first and fourth fingers. You should choose whichever feels more comfortable, but you may find on some other songs you will need use the first and third fingers so you can use the fourth finger to fret other notes.

Pre-chorus (Bars 9–16)

In this arrangement the first half of the pre-chorus is based on the original vocal melody. The second four bars consists of two-note powerchords.

Bars 10–11 | *Alternate Picking*
The first three notes of bar 10 can be played with all down strokes or using alternate picking. However, the remaining notes of bars 9 & 10 should all be played using strict alternate picking starting with an up stroke (Fig. 1) as the tempo of the songs means it would be difficult to play this phrase using single direction picking.

Bars 13–16 | *Moving powerchords*
As you move between the powerchords in the pre-chorus lock your fingers in position and move your whole hand to the next chord. This will make your changes more efficient and, as a result, much faster.

Chorus (Bars 17–23)

The chorus is made up of two-note powerchords some of which are preceded by passing notes played on open strings.

Bars 17–23 | *Complex rhythms*
If you struggle with this section try removing the open strings and playing the basic chords (Fig. 2). Once you can play this comfortably, you will find it easier to embellish the progression with the passing notes played on open strings.

Verse 2 (Bars 25–32)

The first four bars of the second verse consists of the first two beats of the original riff. After three, two-note powerchords the final E minor chord is played in a quarter note rhythm for one bar before the final chord.

Bar 25 | *Fingering options*
The second and third notes can be played with two different fingerings. You can use your fourth finger to play the E note at the 7th fret of the fifth string and use your third finger to play the B note on the 7th fret on the sixth string. If you opt for this fingering make sure the first note does not ring for too long. The other, more challenging, option is to play the E note with the pad of your first finger and 'roll' it onto the tip of the same finger to play the B note. This will eliminate any note value problems.

Bar 25 | *Correct note values*
The last note of the riff is an eighth note. Mute the fifth string to ensure it sounds for the correct note value.

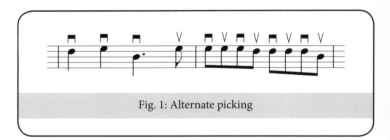

Fig. 1: Alternate picking

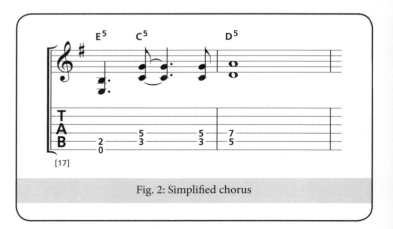

Fig. 2: Simplified chorus

SONG TITLE: RUN TO YOU
ALBUM: RECKLESS
RELEASED: 1984
LABEL: A&M
GENRE: CLASSIC ROCK

PERSONNEL: BRYAN ADAMS (GTR+VOX)
KEITH SCOTT (GTR)
DAVE TAYLOR (BASS)
TOMMY MANDEL (KEYS)
MICKEY CURRY (DRUMS)

UK CHART PEAK: 11
US CHART PEAK: 6

BACKGROUND INFO

'Run To You' was the first single from 1984's *Reckless*. It's built around a repeated riff that gets its distinctive sound from the open fourth string that's repeated in every chord. The original song is played with a capo at the second fret, but sounds just as effective without a capo, as can be seen in the exam version. The chorus uses simple open chords which are the perfect contrast to the rolling arpeggios found in the verse and pre-chorus. The bridge section changes the dynamic further with a breakdown that features a simple repeated motif before the song picks up again with a reprise of the chorus.

THE BIGGER PICTURE

Reckless was Adams' big break. While its predecessor *Cuts Like A Knife* achieved recognition in his native Canada and the U.S., the catchy, radio friendly hits found on *Reckless* secured him global success. Though he released *Into The Fire* in 1987 and a subsequent live album, he didn't achieve the same success again until he teamed up with producer Mutt Lange to record the phenomenally successful *Waking Up The Neighbours* in 1991.

NOTES

The main guitar parts are treated with a chorus effect (probably added post-production). This effect was used widely on guitar parts, particularly picked chordal parts, through the mid-to-late 80s. Def Leppard's *Hysteria* album is probably the most famous example of this tone, particularly the single 'Love Bites'. As with all genres there are a whole host of 'also rans' who imitated this sound. As popular as it was, the chorused guitar tone dated quickly and was largely discarded by the simplistic production values that were associated with the grunge movement of the early 90s. However, you can still hear the chorus effect on Nirvana's *Nevermind*, most notably the main riff to the single 'Come As You Are'.

RECOMMENDED LISTENING

Aside from 'Run To You', *Reckless* contains some of Adams' biggest hits including pub band favourite, 'Summer Of '69' and the U.S. number one 'Heaven'. 1991's *Waking Up The Neighbours* features the raucous 'Can't Stop This Thing We Started' and the mega-hit 'Everything I Do (I Do It For You)' which, Hollywood production aside, features a tasteful guitar solo.

Run To You

Bryan Adams

Words & Music by Bryan Adams & Jim Vallance

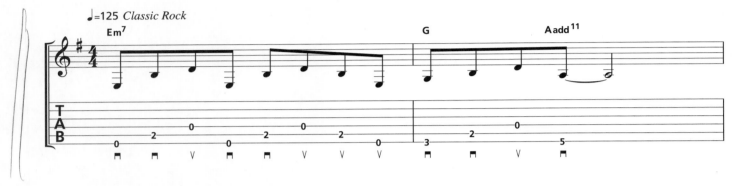

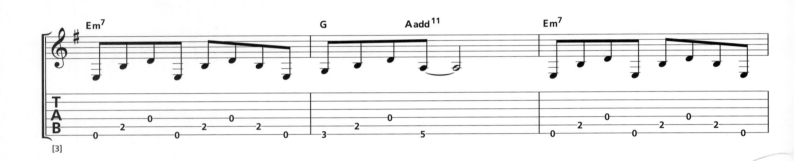

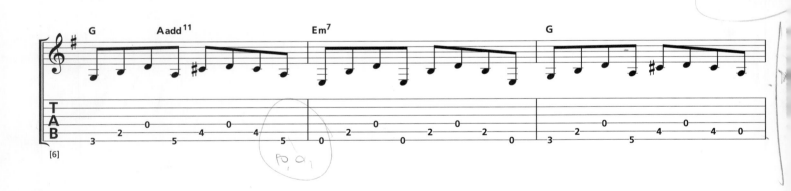

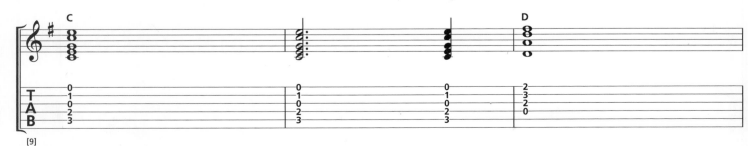

Walkthrough

Tone

Guitar sounds in the 80s were often heavily processed (lots of effects were added) sometimes making use of multiple effects pedals at the same time. While the original version of 'Run To You' uses a chorus effect, you are not expected to use this in Grade 1. A clean sound with the treble boosted will produce a bright rock sound that's perfect for the song, especially the picked rhythm parts. If your guitar is fitted with humbuckers you should use the bridge pickup to get the required sound.

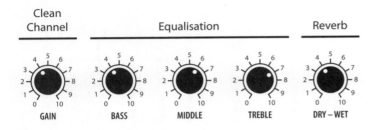

Intro/Verse (Bars 1–8)

This section consists entirely of arpeggios based on a three-chord progression. The first two cycles of this progression end with a sustained A note, while the final two are made up of eighth notes. Although the chord names look quite complex, they are all relatively simple fretboard shapes.

Bars 1–8 | *The 'Next Note' method*

There are many picking options for the main riff. One popular method is the 'Next Note' method. Start with a down stroke, then pick the following notes in the direction that the pick has to travel in order to reach the next note. A consistent picking approach like this will increase fluency.

Bars 1–8 | *Consistent arpeggios*

Aim for a consistent sound when playing these arpeggios where each note is played at the same volume. Watch particularly for the first up stroke in the sequence (the third, sixth and eleventh notes of the riff) as many players have a tendency to play this type of note too hard.

Bar 8 | *Shifting positions*

Instead of playing the final A note of the riff at the 5th fret of the sixth string, play it on the open fifth string. This allows you to move your hand in position to play the pre-chorus chords as you play the open string, eliminating the quick shift at the end of the bar.

Pre-chorus (Bars 9–12)

The pre-chorus uses open chords throughout. It starts with simple rhythms but finishes with a challenging bar that starts on an upbeat.

Bar 12 | *Counting rhythms*

This rhythm is quite challenging, so start slowly as you learn the part and gradually increase the speed. Count the bar in eighth notes ("1 & 2 & 3 & 4 &") and move your picking hand in a constant 'down-up' motion. Fig. 1 shows you where each note should be played in relation to the count.

Chorus (Bars 13–18)

The first four bars of the chorus use open chords played in a syncopated rhythm (this is where the music accents the weaker beats in the bar). The final four bars fill out this basic rhythm with extra chord strums.

Bars 13–15 | *Constant strumming motion*

Keeping your picking hand in a constant motion between the chord hits in bars 13–15 will help the part sound more fluent. Fig. 2 illustrates the strum motions that don't strike strings which are commonly known as 'ghost' strokes.

Bars 17–18 | *Counting long note values*

From a technical point of view playing a sustained chord is fairly straightforward, but make sure you count and/or tap your foot through bar 18. This will help you keep your place in the music and play the first note of bar 19 in time.

Outro (Bars 19–23)

This is a variation of the intro and verse. This time the section starts with the eighth-note version and is followed by the variation with the sustained A note.

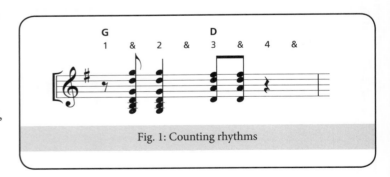

Fig. 1: Counting rhythms

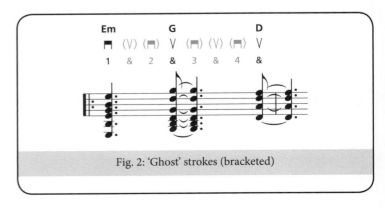

Fig. 2: 'Ghost' strokes (bracketed)

SONG TITLE: SUNSHINE OF YOUR LOVE
ALBUM: DISRAELI GEARS
RELEASED: 1967
LABEL: REACTION
GENRE: BLUES-ROCK

PERSONNEL: ERIC CLAPTON (GTR+VOX)
JACK BRUCE (BASS+VOX)
GINGER BAKER (DRUMS)

UK CHART PEAK: 25
US CHART PEAK: 5

BACKGROUND INFO

The song is based on a two-bar syncopated riff (where the notes are placed on the weaker beats of the bar) that uses the D blues scale. There are two versions of this riff: the single-note version played in unison with the bass guitar in the intro and the version where the first four notes are substituted with chords. After 24 bars in D, the riff moves to G before returning D. This I–IV chord movement is based on the first part of a 12-bar blues progression.

Eric Clapton's guitar solo famously quotes the melody from the classic 'Blue Moon', before moving into more standard blues-rock territory.

THE BIGGER PICTURE

Cream's studio albums were generally made up of concise songs with short, well constructed solos. This was a sharp contrast to their live performances where extended improvisations were a large part of the show. Clapton's later work is restrained in comparison, but it's important to remember that his playing in the 60s was groundbreaking and influenced many guitarists, including Edward Van Halen who likened Cream's improvisational style to 'falling downstairs and landing on their feet', a phrase he used in connection with his own playing. He has also recounted stories of slowing the revolutions of his vinyl record player to hear Clapton's licks at slower speeds so he could transcribe them.

NOTES

Legend has it that one of the band hammered out a clichéd Native American rhythm on the table to drummer Ginger Baker and the thumping tom tom pattern that drives the song was born.

RECOMMENDED LISTENING

Cream's 1966 debut *Fresh Cream* contains 'I Feel Free' which features Clapton's solo that embellishes the vocal melody. *Disraeli Gears* features 'Strange Brew', a funky blues track punctuated with Clapton's tasteful fills between vocal lines. The guitar solo is a fine example of Clapton's early lead style. The live portion of the *Wheels On Fire* release, particularly the 16-minute 'Spoonful', show off the improvisations that Cream were so famous for. In 2005 Cream reformed for a set of live performances. The imaginatively titled *Royal Albert Hall May 2-3-5-6 2005* contains interesting, though relatively pedestrian, versions of their classic songs.

Sunshine Of Your Love

Cream
Words & Music by Jack Bruce, Pete Brown & Eric Clapton

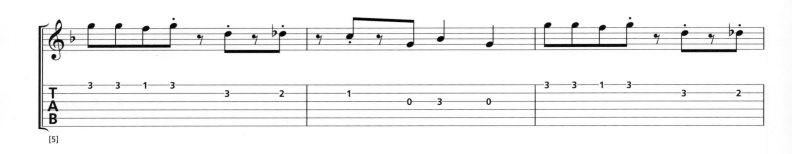

[5]

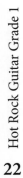

[8]

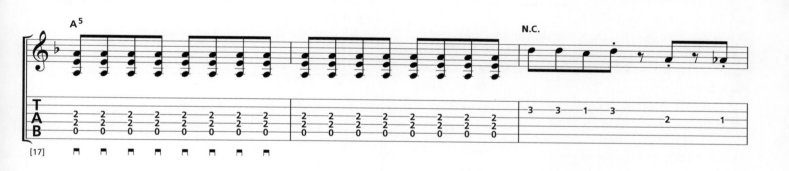

Walkthrough

Tone

Eric Clapton used a Gibson SG through a Marshall, though live videos also show him using a Fender Stratocaster. Aim for an overdriven sound that is aggressive, but still has clarity when the chords are struck aggressively. Boost the middle to help the guitar cut through the rest of the track.

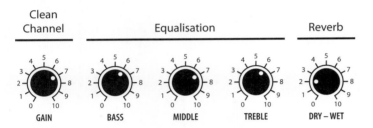

Main Riff 1 (Bars 1–4)

The main riff forms the bulk of the song. It combines syncopated rhythms (when notes are played on the weaker beats of the bar) with staccato (short, detached) phrasing.

Bars 1–12 | *One finger per fret*

The most obvious fingering option for this riff is: first finger plays the 1st fret, the second plays the 2nd fret and the third plays the 3rd fret (Fig. 1). This will reduce unnecessary hand movement and give you an organised, systematic approach to your fingering which will allow you to focus on the other aspects of the performance.

Bar 1 | *Fluent phrasing*

When you start the riff (using the third finger) make sure your first finger is in position on the 1st fret of the first string ready to play the note. Don't not remove it until you have played the D note (at the 3rd fret for the third time). This will make the movement between the first four notes of the riff as smooth as possible.

Bars 1–4 | *Performing staccato notes*

Staccato notes are indicated by a dot above or below the note (Fig. 2) and should be articulated by releasing pressure on the string. Don't take the finger all the way off the string, this will slow you down and produce unwanted string noise, just stop pressing. The open string notes should be muted by placing the pick back on string after playing the note.

Riff Variation (Bars 5–7)

This variation of the riff sounds identical to the preceding four bars but transposed (moved) to a higher pitch. You may have expected that the fingering pattern would be identical to the previous phrase, but it is not – this is because the G and B strings are tuned a 3rd apart, whereas all other strings are a 4th apart.

Main Riff 2 (Bars 9–12)

This is a reprise of the main riff that brings a sense of resolution to the song after the riff variation ready for the chorus.

Chorus (Bars 13–18)

The aggressive on-beat rhythms in the chorus contrast the syncopated main riff. It makes use of both powerchords and open chords. The section builds to climax with a repeated A^5 powerchord that sets up the transition to the main riff.

Bars 13–16 | *Muting chords*

The A chord played on beat 2 of bars 13 and 15 should last for one eighth note. Chords played with a distorted tone will sustain for long periods unless they are controlled. To make sure the chord rings for the correct duration you will need to mute the chord after you have played it. Release the pressure on your fretting fingers, don't take your fingers all the way off the strings, just stop pressing. Simultaneously mute the strings with the edge of your picking hand.

Main Riff 3 (Bars 19–22)

This is the final reprise of the main riff that brings the song to a close.

Bar 22 | *Ending the song cleanly*

Don't allow the final note of the song to ring for longer than the notated quarter note duration. Mute the open string by placing your pick back on the string after the note has sounded for the correct amount of time.

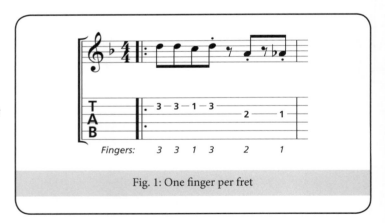

Fig. 1: One finger per fret

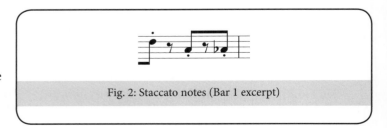

Fig. 2: Staccato notes (Bar 1 excerpt)

```
     SONG TITLE:  WISHING WELL
          ALBUM:  HEARTBREAKER
       RELEASED:  1973
          LABEL:  ISLAND
          GENRE:  CLASSIC ROCK

      PERSONNEL:  PAUL RODGERS (VOX)
                  PAUL KOSSOFF (GTR)
                  JOHN BUNDRICK (KEYS)
                  TETSU YAMAUCHI (BASS)
                  SIMON KIRKE (DRUMS)

UK CHART PEAK:  7
US CHART PEAK:  N/A
```

BACKGROUND INFO

Like all classic rock songs, 'Wishing Well' is based on a simple, yet irrepressible, riff. The verses move between staccato (short, detached) octaves and more flowing powerchord parts. As the song moves into the pseudo choir-laden bridge and guitar solo it changes from E minor to the key of A minor and for the rest of the song the main riff is played in A – higher on the guitar's neck. This gives the music a 'lift' that maintains interest as the song progresses.

THE BIGGER PICTURE

Free's combination of Paul Rodgers' soulful classic rock voice and Paul Kossoff's laid back, effortless guitar playing made Free one of the most successful British bands through the late 60s and early 70s. They released six studio albums, the most successful of which was 1970's *Fire And Water*, which reached number 2 in the UK album charts and contains the hit 'All Right Now'.

NOTES

After Free disbanded, singer Paul Rodgers formed Bad Company (with which he recorded six albums),

while Kossoff went on and recorded a solo album called *Back Street Crawler*, which he subsequently used as the name of his band. Back Street Crawler recorded two albums, *The Band Plays On* (1975) and *2nd Street* (1976). Kossoff died on a plane bound for New York, in his sleep, in 1976 after a long period of drug-related ill-health which had affected his ability to perform both live and in the studio throughout his time with Free and Back Street Crawler. He is commemorated by a plaque at Golders Green Crematorium that simply reads 'All right now'.

RECOMMENDED LISTENING

1970's *Fire And Water* contains some of Free's most famous songs. The title track and 'Mr Big' are fine examples of their blues-based rock. 'All Right Now' is a genuine rock guitar classic and its extended guitar solo is an excellent example of Kossoff's tasteful playing and is a great study in constructing a solo. It starts with simple phrases that make use of bends and slides, before climaxing with a fast, high register hammer-on lick and some blistering bends. 1971 single 'My Brother Jake', shows Kossoff in a more supportive role, provided a gentle chordal accompaniment to the main piano part and adding the occasional fill to augment the vocal.

Wishing Well

Free

Words & Music by Paul Rodgers, Simon Kirke, Tetsu Yamauchi, John Bundrick & Paul Kossoff

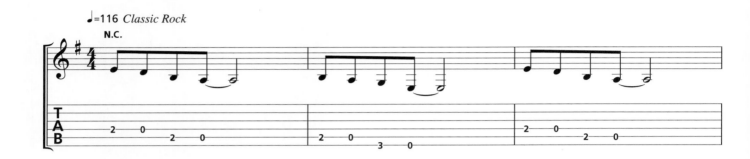

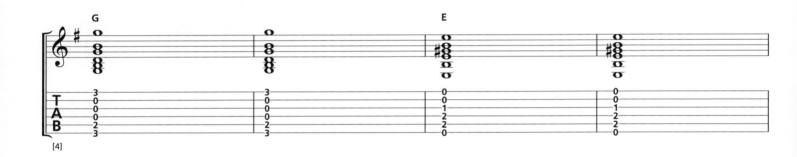

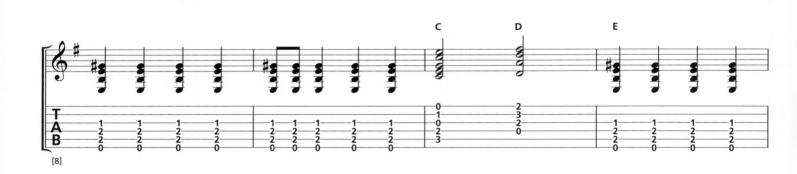

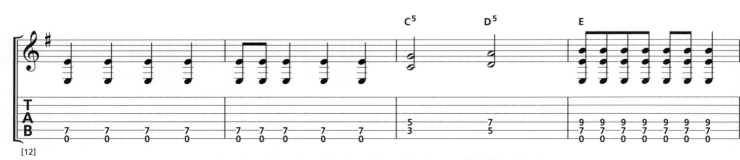

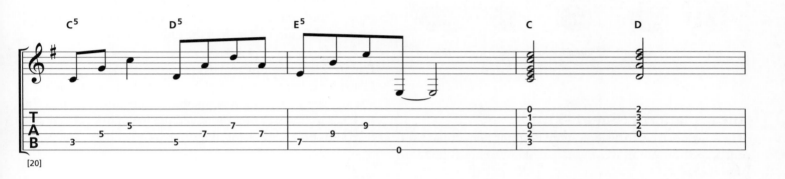

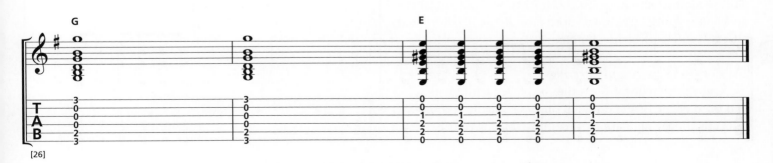

Walkthrough

Tone

Like a lot of classic rock songs, the tone on 'Wishing Well' is the product of the humbucker-loaded Gibson Les Paul played through a Marshall amplifier. If you have a guitar with single coil pickups use the pickup nearest the neck to get a full, warm sound. While the sound is quite heavily overdriven, using too much gain or a modern distortion will compromise the guitar's clarity.

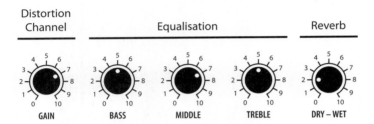

Intro/main riff (Bars 1–7)

The song opens with a single-note E minor pentatonic riff in open position and moves to sustained open chords that lead into the verse.

Bars 1–3 | *One finger per fret*
While it's possible to play this section with a single finger, use either your first and second or second and third fingers to play this riff (Fig. 1). This will keep your fingering organised – a good habit to develop for when you attempt more challenging material.

Bars 1–3 | *Fretting accuracy*
Make sure you keep your fingers as close to the frets as possible without physically being on top of them, as this will help you avoid fret-buzz.

Bar 10 | *Strumming accuracy*
Although this bar is rhythmically straightforward, take care not to play any unwanted strings as this will affect the clarity of the part. If you find it difficult to hear whether you are hitting the right strings, you can check this without looking at your picking hand by watching to see if the unwanted strings are vibrating.

Verse (Bars 8–15)

This section starts with open chords then moves to octaves and powerchords. The final chord is an E^5 powerchord with an 'extra' low sixth string, E note.

Bars 14–16 | *Powerchord fingerings*
Two-note powerchords can either be played with the first and third or the first and fourth fingers. Usually you should select the fingering that's most comfortable for your hand

size, but in this case it may be advisable to use your first and third fingers as this will aid a smooth transition to the three-note powerchords in the chorus section.

Chorus (Bars 16–22)

This section is based on powerchords. They are either strummed or arpeggiated (each note played separately), and finishes with open chords leading into the main riff/outro.

Bars 16–17 | *Moving between powerchords*
Think of the C^5, D^5 and E^5 chords as a single shape that is moved around the fretboard. Lock your hand into the powerchord shape when you play the C^5 chord then move your whole hand rather than the individual fingers.

Bar 16–21 | *Picking arpeggios*
Consider using the 'Next Note' method. Start with a down stroke, then pick the following notes in the direction that the pick has to travel in order to reach the next note. This may help with the tricky string skips in bars 19 and 21 (Fig. 2).

Outro/main riff (Bars 23–29)

This is a variation of the intro. The main riff is identical, but the first bar final E chord is played in quarter note rhythm to help bring the song to a climax on the final chord.

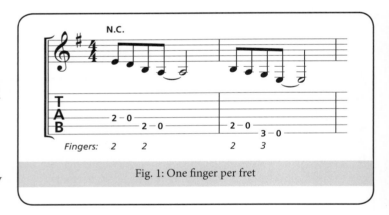

Fig. 1: One finger per fret

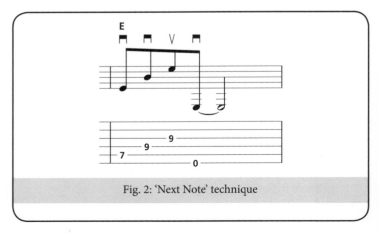

Fig. 2: 'Next Note' technique

SONG TITLE: WONDERFUL TONIGHT
ALBUM: SLOWHAND
RELEASED: 1977
LABEL: RSO
GENRE: ROCK

PERSONNEL: ERIC CLAPTON (VOX +GTR)
CARL RADLE (BASS)
JAMIE OLDAKER (DRUMS)
DICK SIMS (KEYS)

UK CHART PEAK: N/A
US CHART PEAK: 60

BACKGROUND INFO

'Wonderful Tonight' was a single (un-released in the UK) from the 1977 album *Slowhand*. 'Slowhand' is Eric Clapton's nickname: an ironic reference to his fast fingers derived from the slow clapping bored audiences use to jeer bands (slow hand clap[ton]). While it wasn't a hit when first released, 'Wonderful Tonight' is a perennial live favourite and a constant feature in the setlists of function bands the world over.

'Wonderful Tonight' is a rock ballad. The arrangement is based on two simple chord progressions that are played using arpeggiated chords (each note of the chord is picked individually). The song's main hook is the catchy major scale melody that is stated throughout the song.

THE BIGGER PICTURE

Much is made of Clapton's lead playing, but a big part of his commercial success are the songs, particularly the memorable riffs, he writes. Songs like 'Bad Love' (co-written with Foreigner guitarist Mick Jones) and the acoustic ballad 'Tears In Heaven' feature memorable riffs and catchy choruses that make Clapton's music highly digestible and has helped him avoid appealing to a 'guitarists only' audience - unlike a lot of his peers.

NOTES

'Wonderful Tonight' is written about Clapton's lover, Pattie Boyd while he was waiting for her to get ready (note the impatient slant to the lyrics in the first verse). 'Wonderful Tonight' isn't the first song he wrote about her. 'Layla' from 1970's *Layla and Assorted Love Songs* was written about his unrequited love for Boyd, who, at the time, was married to another guitar legend: George Harrison.

RECOMMENDED LISTENING

Clapton's later material sees him moving away from his middle-of-the-road rock music and back towards his blues roots. 1994's *From The Cradle* was a collection of blues covers. Of particular note are 'I'm Tore Down', which sees Clapton return to the fiery blues-rock playing that he made his name with in Cream. There's also his version of Freddie King's ballad 'Someday After A While (You'll Be Sorry)' which showcases Clapton's tasteful phrasing. In 2004 Clapton recorded 'Me and Mr Johnson', which featured re-working's of a selection of blues legend Robert Johnson's small, but immensely influential recordings. One standout track is the ragtime influenced 'They're Red Hot'.

Wonderful Tonight

Eric Clapton
Words & Music by Eric Clapton

[5]

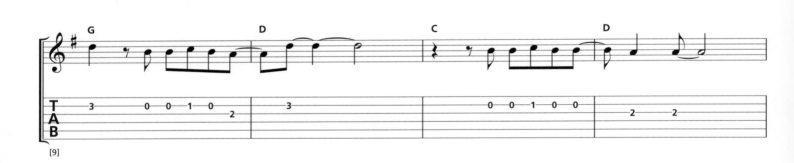

[9]

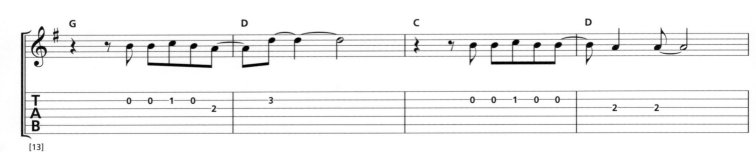

[13]

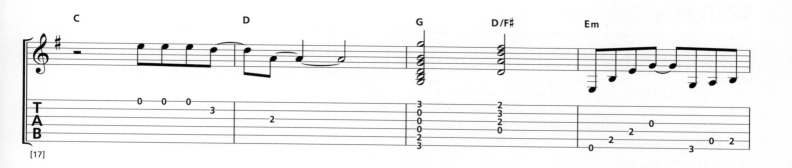

[17]

[21]

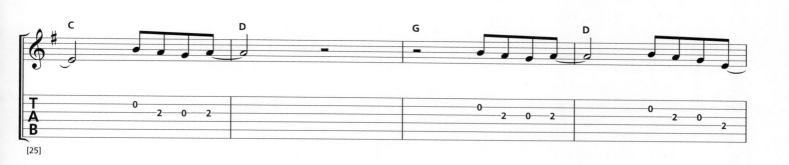

[25]

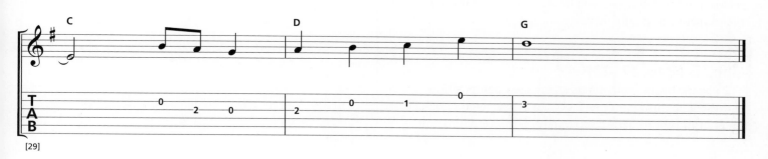

[29]

Walkthrough

Tone

This arrangement uses lots of the higher pitched open strings. These have a tendency to sound thin, so aim for a full, warm tone. If your guitar is fitted with singlecoils, opt for the pickup located near the neck. Adding some reverb (if you have it) will add atmosphere to the performance and help the longer notes sustain, but be wary of adding too much as this will swamp the notes and affect clarity.

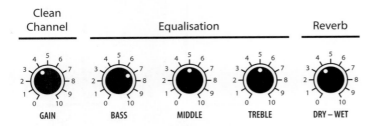

Intro Melody (Bars 1–9)

This section is an open position (open strings and first four frets) version of the original's lead guitar melody. The eight-bar melody consists of a four-note motif where the final note follows the chords in the accompaniment. The final two bars end with an ascending line that finishes on the first beat of the first bar of the verse.

Bar 8 | *Timing*

Playing in time at a slow tempo is more difficult than it seems. Although technically this bar is straightforward, take care not to rush the notes and play them ahead of the beat.

Verse (Bars 9–16)

This section is an arrangement based on Eric Clapton's original vocal melody. It's a single-note open position melody in the key of G major. It starts on an upbeat and features a rhythm that emphasises the weaker beats (Fig. 1). This is known as 'syncopation'.

Bars 11 – 12 | *Counting rhythms*

These bars feature a tricky syncopated rhythm that looks complicated on paper, but can be learned by ear by listening to the full recording. Alternatively you can count the bar in eighth notes (1 & 2 & 3 & 4 &) at a slow tempo and play the notes on the correct beats. Fig. 1 shows the melody in relation to the count. As you become more comfortable with the phrasing gradually increase the speed.

Chorus (Bars 17–23)

The chorus begins with single strums of open position chords. The third bar opens with an arpeggiated (single notes of the chord played separately) E minor chord and

ends with a three-note ascending scalic phrase that leads into the, somewhat more challenging, open position arpeggios in bars 21 and 22.

Bar 19 | *Strumming accuracy*

Playing the six string G chord is straightforward, but take care not play any unwanted strings on the D chord.

Bar 20 | *Picking options*

There are two options for picking the final three notes of bar 20. Ideally the following bar should start with a down stroke, so you should either pick the three notes in bar 20 with consecutive down strokes or use alternate picking starting with an up stroke (Fig. 2).

Bars 21–23 | *Playing arpeggios*

This is undoubtedly the most challenging part of the song. Make sure you use an organised picking approach that is consistent and stays the same every time you play the part. One option, the 'Next Note' method, is outlined on page 30. Start slowly and break the two bars down into two-beat chunks, once you feel more comfortable join the two beats together and work on a bar at a time.

Outro (Bars 23–31)

The outro is a reprise of the intro melody that brings the song to a close.

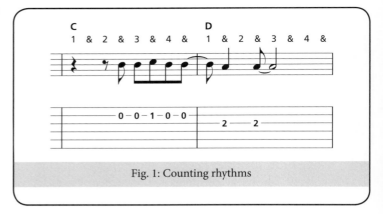

Fig. 1: Counting rhythms

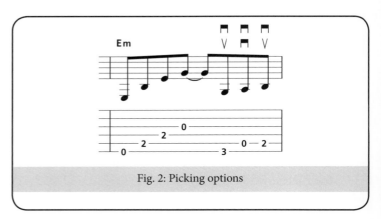

Fig. 2: Picking options

Red Hot Chili Peppers

SONG TITLE: ZEPHYR SONG
ALBUM: BY THE WAY
RELEASED: 2002
LABEL: WARNER BROS.
GENRE: ALTERNATIVE ROCK

PERSONNEL: ANTHONY KIEDIS (VOX)
JOHN FRUSCIANTE (GTR)
FLEA (BASS)
CHAD SMITH (DRUMS)

UK CHART PEAK: 11
US CHART PEAK: 49

BACKGROUND INFO

'The Zephyr Song' was the second single from the 2002 release *By The Way*. It follows a familiar format to a lot of Chili Peppers' songs such as 'Californication' and 'By The Way', where the verses are built on a repeated catchy riff while the choruses make use of simple strummed open chords to allow room for Anthony Kiedis' vocal.

THE BIGGER PICTURE

Like a lot of bands that have been successful for a long time, the Chili Peppers' sound has gradually evolved. They started life as a wild funk-rock outfit centred around Flea's hyperactive slap basslines and Kiedis's rap-influenced vocals. After the death of their original guitarist, Hillel Slovak, John Frusciante (himself a lifelong fan of the band) was drafted in as replacement. He introduced a different take on the Chili Peppers' funk sound, adding Leo Noncentelli-influenced single-note lines and more pronounced variations in dynamics to *Mother's Milk* and *Blood Sugar Sex Magik*. The Chili Peppers have continued this process of maturation towards a more 'straight' rock sound, with their trademark funk stylings making less frequent, more controlled appearances in their latest work.

NOTES

Although John Frusicante played on five albums with the Chili Peppers, they recorded *One Hot Minute* with former Jane's Addiction guitarist Dave Navarro in between *Blood Sugar Sex Magik* and *Californication*. Frusciante left the band in 1992 (reportedly struggling with drug addiction) before returning in 1998. *One Hot Minute* was a more straight-ahead rock album as Navarro was not comfortable playing funk. While it contained hits like 'Aeroplane' and 'My Friends', it is now largely ignored by band, media and fans alike. John Frusciante left the band again in 2009.

RECOMMENDED LISTENING

The Chili Peppers' discography falls into three distinct phases. From their early, frenetic albums *The Uplift Mofo Party Plan* contains 'Backwoods', 'Fight Like A Brave' and the Beatles-influenced 'Behind The Sun'. The first Frusciante period features the outstanding *Blood Sugar Sex Magik* which contains the funk-rock classic 'Suck My Kiss', dance floor favourite 'Give It Away' and mega-hit 'Under The Bridge'. The second, mellower, Frusciante period yielded *Californication* which contains the hits 'Scar Tissue' and the acoustic gem 'Road Trippin'.

Zephyr Song

Red Hot Chili Peppers

Words & Music by Anthony Kiedis, Flea, John Frusciante & Chad Smith

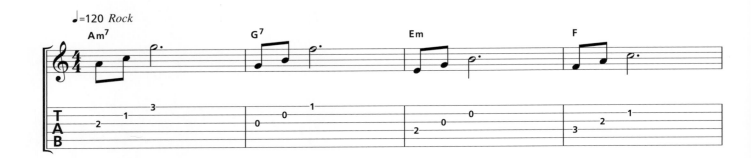

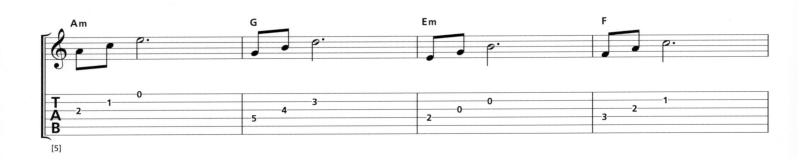

[5]

[9]

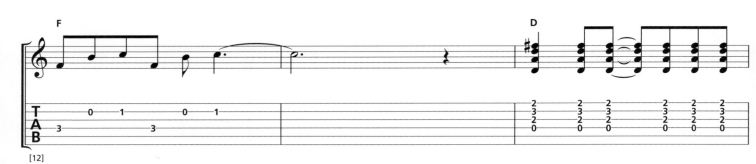

[12]

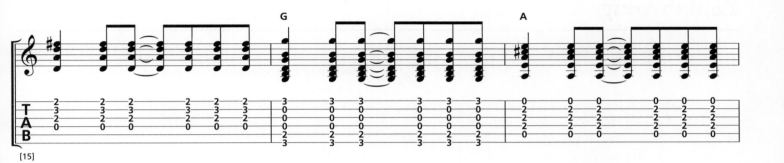

Walkthrough

Tone

Live videos of the 'Zephyr Song' show John Frusciante using a Fender Stratocaster through a Marshall amp. You should aim for a warm, well-rounded clean tone. If you have a guitar fitted with singlecoils, use the pickup nearest the bridge to get the warmest sound. Guitars fitted with humbuckers should use the bridge pickup to avoid the chords sounding too muddy in the chorus. Avoid the temptation to add too much reverb as this can swamp the sound, especially in the strummed sections.

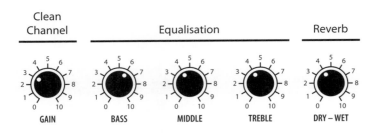

Intro (Bars 1–8)

The section uses arpeggiated chords (each note of the chord is played separately). The second half of the riff is a variation of the first that uses different versions of the Am and G chords.

Bars 1–8 | *Fretting Accuracy*

Ensure that you play on the tips of your fingers so you don't mute the highest strings. If you find this difficult, examine the position of your thumb as this can sometimes restrict your finger motion.

Verse 1 | *Bars 9–13*

The verse uses the same chords as the intro, but is a more melodic part that starts with the 'root' note of the chord held for two beats and is followed by a short phrase using the A natural minor scale. The root is the note that gives the chord its name, for example, the root note of an A minor chord is 'A', and the root of a D major chord is 'D'.

Bars 9–11 | *Correct Note Values*

Make sure the half notes at the beginning of each bar don't ring on into the third and fourth beats. This will not only cause clashes with the subsequent melodic passages it will also make them more difficult to play

Bars 9–13 | *Alternate Picking*

While there are no examination requirements specifying which picking patterns you should follow, it is important to use a picking technique that produces a fluent and consistent performance. The melodic lines in these four bars are quite challenging at this tempo, so alternate picking (sticking strictly to a 'down up down up' picking pattern) is the most efficient picking action (Fig. 1).

Chorus (Bars 14–21)

The chorus is split into two sections, the first 4 bars are strummed open chords and the remaining 8 bars are an arrangement of the original vocal part.

Bars 14–17 | *Constant Strumming Motion*

Your strumming hand should move in a constant eighth note motion. It should not stop when it's not striking the strings as this will hinder fluency.

Bars 18–21 | *'Predictive' Fingerings*

If this section was played in isolation then any two-finger combination would be acceptable. However, the reprise of the verse that follows should start with the first note played with the second finger. To prepare for this you should play this section with your second and third fingers (Fig. 2).

Verse 2 (Bars 22–26)

This slight variation of the first verse and brings the song to an end with a sustained A minor chord.

Bars 25–26 | *Smooth transitions*

At the end the of bar 25 your first finger is already in place to play the subsequent A minor chord. Practise by starting with just your first finger on the first fret of the second string and then adding the remaining two fingers that make up the rest of the chord. This will reduce excessive motion and make a smoother transition to the songs final chord.

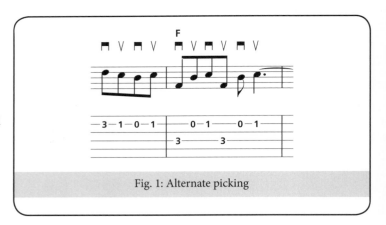

Fig. 1: Alternate picking

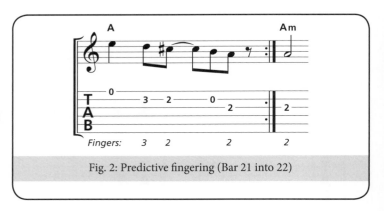

Fig. 2: Predictive fingering (Bar 21 into 22)

Guitar Notation Explained

THE MUSICAL STAVE shows pitches and rhythms and is divided by lines into bars. Pitches are named after the first seven letters of the alphabet.

TABLATURE graphically represents the guitar fingerboard. Each horizontal line represents a string and each number represents a fret.

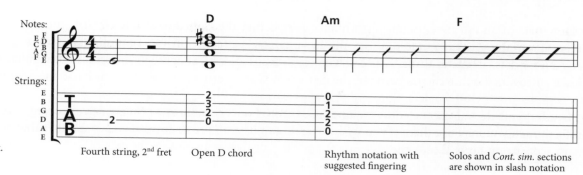

Fourth string, 2nd fret   Open D chord   Rhythm notation with suggested fingering   Solos and *Cont. sim.* sections are shown in slash notation

Definitions For Special Guitar Notation

HAMMER-ON: Pick the lower note, then sound the higher note by fretting it without picking.

PULL-OFF: Pick the higher note then sound the lower note by lifting the finger without picking.

SLIDE: Pick the first note and slide to the next. If the line connects (as below) the second note is *not* repicked.

GLISSANDO: Slide off of a note at the end of its rhythmic value. The note that follows *is* repicked.

STRING BENDS: Pick the first note then bend (or release the bend) to the pitch indicated in brackets.

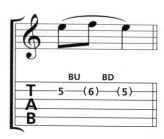

VIBRATO: Vibrate the note by bending and releasing the string smoothly and continuously.

TRILL: Rapidly alternate between the two bracketed notes by hammering on and pulling off.

NATURAL HARMONICS: Lightly touch the string above the indicated fret then pick to sound a harmonic.

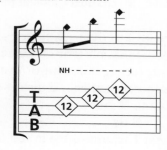

PINCHED HARMONICS: Bring the thumb of the picking hand into contact with the string immediately after the pick.

PICK-HAND TAP: Strike the indicated note with a finger from the picking hand. Usually followed by a pull-off.

FRET-HAND TAP: As pick-hand tap, but use fretting hand. Usually followed by a pull-off or hammer-on.

QUARTER-TONE BEND: Pick the note indicated and bend the string up by a quarter tone.

PRE-BENDS: Before picking the note, bend the string from the fret indicated between the staves, to the equivalent pitch indicated in brackets in the TAB.

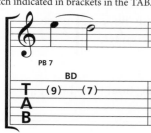

WHAMMY BAR BEND: Use the whammy bar to bend notes to the pitches indicated in brackets in the TAB.

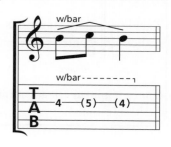

D.%. al Coda

D.C. al Fine

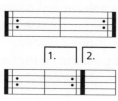

- Go back to the sign (%), then play until the bar marked **To Coda** ✛ then skip to the section marked ✛ **Coda**.

- Go back to the beginning of the song and play until the bar marked **Fine** (end).

- Repeat the bars between the repeat signs.

- When a repeated section has different endings, play the first ending only the first time and the second ending only the second time.

Introduction to Tone

A large part of an effective guitar performance is selecting the right tone. The electric guitar's sound is subject to a wide range of variables. This guide outlines the basic controls present on most amplifiers as well as the common variations between models. There is also a basic overview of pickups and the effect their location on the guitar has on the guitar's tone. Finally, it covers the differences between the distortion types – crucial to getting your basic sound right.

At Grade 1 you are only expected to use one tone throughout the song and you are not expected to use any additional effects units, though you may use them if you wish. You do not have to use distortion and remember that at Grade 1 a performance on an acoustic guitar is acceptable.

Basic amplifier controls

Most amplifiers come with a standard set of controls that are the same as, or very similar to, the diagram below. It's important to understand what each control is and the effect it has on your guitar's tone.

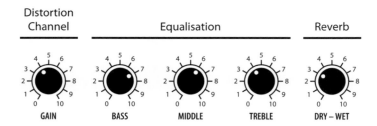

- **Channel (Clean/Distortion)**

  Most amplifiers have two channels, which can be selected by either a switch on the amp or a footswitch. One channel is usually 'clean' while the other can be driven harder to create a distorted (or 'dirty') tone. If your amp doesn't have two channels, look at the 'variation of basic controls' to see how to get clean and dirty tones from a one channel amp.

- **Gain**

  In simple terms the gain determines how hard you drive the amp. This governs how distorted the dirty (also called 'drive', 'overdrive' or 'distortion') channel is and acts as a second volume control on the clean channel (though a high gain setting will distort even the clean channel).

- **Bass**

  This adjusts the lowest frequencies. Boost it to add warmth and reduce or 'cut' it if your sound is muddy or woolly.

- **Middle**

  This is the most important equalisation (often shortened to just 'EQ') control. Most of the guitar's tone character is found in the midrange, so adjusting this control has a lot of impact on your tone. Boosting it with a dirty sound will give a more classic rock sound, while cutting it will produce a more metal tone.

- **Treble**

  This adjusts the high frequencies. Boost it to add brightness and cut it if the sound is too harsh or brittle.

- **Reverb**

  Short for 'reverberation'. This artificially recreates the ambience of your guitar in a large room, usually a hall. This dial controls the balance between the 'dry' (the sound without the reverb) and 'wet' (the sound with the reverb) sounds.

Variations of basic controls

The diagram above shows the most common amp controls. There are many variations to this basic setup which can be confusing. The following section is a breakdown of some of the other amp controls you may encounter.

- **Presence control**

  Sometimes this dial replaces the 'middle' control and sometimes it appears in addition to it. It adjusts the higher midrange frequencies (those found between the 'middle' and 'treble' dials).

- **No reverb control**

  Reverb can be a nice addition to your guitar tone, but it is not essential. Don't be concerned if your amp does not have a reverb control.

- **Volume, gain, master setup**

  Single channel amplifiers often have an extra volume control (in addition to the master volume) located next to the gain control. For clean sounds keep the gain set low and the volume similarly low and use the master control for overall volume. If the master control is on 10 and you require more level, turn the volume control up, though you may find this starts to distort as you reach the higher numbers.

  To get a distorted tone turn the volume down low and the gain up till you get the amount of distortion you require. Regulate the overall level with master volume. As before, if the master control is on 10 and you require more level, turn the volume up. In this case, however, you may find you lose clarity before you reach maximum.

Pickups

Entire books have been devoted to the intricacies of pickups. However, three basic pieces of information will help you understand a lot about your guitar tone:

- **Singlecoils**

  Singlecoils are narrow pickups that you'll see fitted to many guitars. The Fender Stratocaster is the most famous guitar fitted with singlecoils. They produce a bright, cutting sound that can sound a little thin in some situations, especially heavier styles of rock music.

- **Humbuckers**

  Humbuckers were originally designed to remove or 'buck' the hum produced by singlecoil pickups, hence the name 'humbuckers'. They produce a warm, mellow sound compared to singlecoil pickups, but have a tendency to sound a little muddy in some situations. They are usually identifiable because they are twice the width of a singlecoil pickup. The Gibson Les Paul is a well-known guitar that is fitted with humbucking pickups.

- **Pickup location**

  Pickups located near the guitar's neck will have the warmest sound, while pickups located near the bridge will have the brightest sound.

Different types of 'dirty' tones

There are lots of different words to describe the 'dirty' guitar sounds. In fact, all the sounds are 'distortions' of the clean tone, which can be confusing when you consider there's a 'type' of distortion called 'distortion'! Below is a simplified breakdown of the three main types of dirty sounds and some listening material to help you through this tonal minefield.

- **Overdrive**

  This is the 'mildest' form of distortion. It can be quite subtle and only evident when the guitar is played strongly. It can be also be full-on and aggressive.
  Hear it on: Cream – 'Sunshine Of Your Love', AC/DC – 'Back In Black', Oasis – 'Cigarettes and Alcohol'.

- **Distortion**

  Distortion is usually associated with heavier styles of music. It is dense and the most extreme of the dirty tones and usually associated with heavy styles of music.
  Hear it on: Metallica – 'Enter Sandman', Avenged Sevenfold – 'Bat Country', Bon Jovi – 'You Give Love A Bad Name'.

- **Fuzz**

  As the name implies fuzz is a broken, 'fuzzy' sound. It was very popular in the 60s, but while still popular, is less common now.
  Hear it on: Jimi Hendrix Experience – 'Purple Haze', The Kinks – 'You Really Got Me'.

Free Choice Pieces, Entering Exams and Marking schemes

Free Choice Pieces

The songs featured in Hot Rock are arranged for use as free choice pieces in Rockschool exams. In the grade exams you can play up to two tracks from this book alongside one choice from the Rockschool Grade 1 book. If you are taking the Performance Certificate exam you may play up to three tracks from this book alongside two choices from the Rockschool Grade 1 book.

Entering Exams

Entering a Rockschool exam is easy. You may enter online at *www.rockschool.co.uk* or by downloading and filling in an exam entry form. The full Rockschool examination terms and conditions as well as exam periods and current fees are available from our website or by calling +44 (0)845 460 4747.

Marking Schemes

Below are the marking schemes for the two different types of Rockschool exam.

GRADE EXAMS | GRADES 1–5

ELEMENT	PASS	MERIT	DISTINCTION
Performance Piece 1	12–14 out of 20	15–17 out of 20	18+ out of 20
Performance Piece 2	12–14 out of 20	15–17 out of 20	18+ out of 20
Performance Piece 3	12–14 out of 20	15–17 out of 20	18+ out of 20
Technical Exercises	9–10 out of 15	11–12 out of 15	13+ out of 15
Either **Sight Reading** *or* **Improvisation & Interpretation**	6 out of 10	7–8 out of 10	9+ out of 10
Ear Tests	6 out of 10	7–8 out of 10	9+ out of 10
General Musicianship Questions	3 out of 5	4 out of 5	5 out of 5
TOTAL MARKS	**60%+**	**74%+**	**90%+**

PERFORMANCE CERTIFICATES | GRADES 1–8

ELEMENT	PASS	MERIT	DISTINCTION
Performance Piece 1	12–14 out of 20	15–17 out of 20	18+ out of 20
Performance Piece 2	12–14 out of 20	15–17 out of 20	18+ out of 20
Performance Piece 3	12–14 out of 20	15–17 out of 20	18+ out of 20
Performance Piece 4	12–14 out of 20	15–17 out of 20	18+ out of 20
Performance Piece 5	12–14 out of 20	15–17 out of 20	18+ out of 20
TOTAL MARKS	**60%+**	**75%+**	**90%+**

Copyright Information

Audio Copyright

Chasing Cars
(Lightbody/Connolly/Simpson/Wilson/Quinn)
Universal Music Publishing Limited.

Jailbreak
(Lynott)
Universal Music Publishing Limited.

Livin' On A Prayer
(Bon Jovi/Sambora/Child)
Universal Music Publishing Limited /Sony/ATV Music
Publishing.

Run To You
(Adams/Vallance)
Rondor Music International.

Sunshine Of Your Love
(Bruce/Brown/Clapton)
Warner/Chappell Music Limited/Copyright Control.

Wishing Well
(Rodgers/Kirke/Yamauchi/Bundrick/Kossoff)
Universal/Island Music Limited.

Wonderful Tonight
(Clapton)
Copyright Control.

The Zephyr Song
(Kiedis/Flea/Frusciante/Smith)
Moebetoblame Music, USA.

mcps

Photographic Rights

Gary Lightbody – Snow Patrol
Page 5
Focka
flickr.com/photos/focka
CC BY-ND 2.0 License

Scott Gorham – Thin Lizzy
Page 9
Richard Marchewka
flickr.com/photos/rmarchewka
CC BY-SA 2.0 License

Richie Sambora – Bon Jovi
Page 13
Alberto Carrasco Casado
flickr.com/photos/albertocarrasco
CC BY 2.0 License

Bryan Adams – Bryan Adams
Page 17
Marco Maas
flickr.com/photos/qnibert
CC BY 2.0 License

Eric Clapton – Cream
Page 21
F. Antolin Hernandez
flickr.com/photos/f_antolin
CC BY 2.0 License

Paul Kossoff – Free
Page 25
© Ian Dickson/REX

Eric Clapton – Eric Clapton
Page 29
ultomatt
flickr.com/photos/ultomatt
CC BY 2.0 License

John Frusciante – Red Hot Chilli Peppers
Page 33
Rafael Amado Deras
flickr.com/photos/rafamado
CC BY 2.0 License

QUALIFICATIONS

Our practical diplomas are the next step for any Grade 8 musician wanting to start a career in teaching or performance

Music Teaching Diploma
Level 4

Music Teaching Licentiate
Level 6

Teaching Diplomas
are for self-employed teachers who want to develop their skills, or musicians who want to go into music education

Music Performance Diploma
Level 4

Music Performance Licentiate
Level 6

Performance Diplomas
are for artists who wish to develop their existing performance skills and learn about the business and marketing side to being an independent artist

VOCATIONAL QUALIFICATIONS

Our vocational qualifications offer practical structured learning with the flexibility to specialise in different areas of the music industry.

Available at Levels 1–4. Vocational Qualifications are a real alternative to GCSE, A–Level and BTECs.

Music Practitioners
opens the door to all aspects of the music industry from composition and performance to business and technology

Creative Practitioners
provides structured support for artists wanting to develop themselves and get started in the industry

Play the music you love AND get a qualification

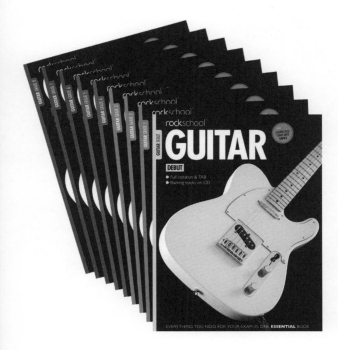

Rockschool Grade books come with everything you need to take the exam.

- **Debut to Grade 8**
- **Six original songs**
- **Standard notation**
- **TAB**
- **CD with full mixes and backing tracks**
- **Examples of the unseen tests**
- **Walkthroughs for every track**

All our grades are accredited by OfQual, and Grades 6, 7 and 8 are worth UCAS points.

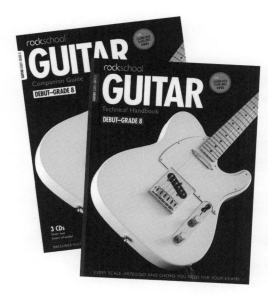

Technical Handbooks & Companion Guides

Rockschool Companion Guides and Technical Handbooks are your essential study guides. Perfect for teachers and students, they are the best way to improve exam performance and technical ability.

LET'S ROCK
START PLAYING NOW!